INDONESIA

TRISTAN BURTON

Facts On File, Inc.

TITLES IN THE COUNTRIES OF THE WORLD SERIES:

ARGENTINA • AUSTRALIA • BRAZIL • CANADA • CHILE
CHINA • EGYPT • FRANCE • GERMANY • INDIA • INDONESIA
ITALY • JAPAN • KENYA • MEXICO • NIGERIA • POLAND
RUSSIA • SOUTH KOREA • SPAIN • SWEDEN • UNITED KINGDOM
UNITED STATES • VIETNAM

Indonesia

Copyright © 2006 by Evans Brothers Limited

Facts On File, Inc.
132 West 31st Street
New York NY 10001

Burton, Tristan.
    Indonesia / Tristan Burton.
        p. cm. — (Countries of the world)
    Includes index.
    Contents: Introducing Indonesia — History of Indonesia up to 1945 — Modern history and politics — Landscape and climate — The economy — People of Indonesia — Conflict and reconciliation — Daily life — The environment — Looking ahead.
    ISBN 0-8160-6016-9
    1. Indonesia—Juvenile literature. I. Title. II. Countries of the world (Facts on File, Inc.)

DS615.B785 2005
959.8—DC22   2005050820

Printed in China by Leo Paper Products Ltd.

10 9 8 7 6 5 4 3 2 1

Editor: Clare Weaver
Designer: Mayer Media Ltd.
Picture researchers: Lynda Lines and Frances Bailey
Map artwork: Peter Bull
Charts and graphs: Encompass Graphics Ltd.

First published by Evans Brothers Limited, 2A Portman Mansions, Chiltern Street, London W1U 6NR, United Kingdom.

This edition published under license from Evans Brothers Limited. All rights reserved.

Endpapers (front): Friday prayers at Mesjid Istiqlal in Jakarta. It is the largest mosque in Indonesia.
Title page: Buyers and sellers at a market in Denpasar, Bali.
Imprint and Contents pages: Boats at the jetty on Gili Trawangan, a small island off Lombok.
Endpapers (back): Irrigated rice terraces, Bali.

INTRODUCING INDONESIA   8

HISTORY OF INDONESIA UP TO 1945   10

MODERN HISTORY AND POLITICS   12

LANDSCAPE AND CLIMATE   14

THE ECONOMY   20

PEOPLE OF INDONESIA   30

CONFLICT AND RECONCILIATION   36

DAILY LIFE   38

THE ENVIRONMENT   46

LOOKING AHEAD   54

GLOSSARY   58

FURTHER INFORMATION   59

INDEX   60

The colors of the Indonesian flag represent palm sugar (red), and rice (white).

Famed for its beaches and coral reefs, Indonesia also has much more to offer.

Indonesia in Southeast Asia is the world's largest archipelago (group of islands). The 17,508 islands stretch from the Indian to the Pacific Oceans, crossing the equator and bridging the continents of Asia and Australia. It has the world's fourth-largest population – 212 million – and the largest Muslim population of any country in the world. It is a country with an amazing diversity of landscapes, people and wildlife.

Indonesia shares 2,830km of land borders with Malaysia, East Timor and Papua New Guinea. It extends around 5,150km from east to west, and 2,012km from north to south. Volcanoes form the backbone to the country, running down from Sumatra through to Nusa Tenggara before looping around through Maluku and Sulawesi. It is one of the most volcanically active countries in the world, forming part of the Pacific "Ring of Fire" (see page 14).

A YOUNG NATION

Inhabiting 6,000 of the archipelago's islands, the people of Indonesia are diverse, with over

A *gamelan* orchestra on Bali. *Gamelan* is the traditional form of Indonesian music.

300 different ethnic groups and more than 350 languages. However, they all form one nation, with one official language, Bahasa Indonesian. For over 300 years the Dutch ruled the islands, then known as the Dutch East Indies, and Indonesia only gained independence from the Netherlands in 1949.

Indonesia remains a country of contrasts. There are vast differences between the islands. Papua has a population density of only 6 people per square kilometer, whereas the island of Java, which makes up only 7 percent of the total land area, has a staggering 59 percent of the population. The government has tried to move people from Java to the other islands, but this has sometimes led to violence between different ethnic communities. There are many inequalities within Indonesia, between the rich and the poor, and between urban and rural areas. Although poverty is declining it is still a major problem that needs to be solved. Many aspects of daily life are gradually getting better for people in Indonesia, but there is still a long way to go.

Indonesia has a wealth of natural resources, including oil, gas, coal, metals and forest products. It is unique in its diversity of Asian and Australian plants and animals. The challenge facing Indonesia is how to develop its economy while at the same time protecting its environment. Industrial pollution, illegal logging, poaching and the destruction of habitats are some of the major environmental problems threatening Indonesia today.

KEY DATA

Official Name:	Republic of Indonesia
Area:	1,919,440km²
Population:	211,559,000 (2000 census)
Official Language:	Bahasa Indonesian
Main Cities:	Jakarta (Java; capital), Surabaya (Java), Bandung (Java), Medan (Sumatra), Semarang (Java), Palembang (Sumatra)
GDP Per Capita:	US$3,361*
Currency:	Indonesian rupiah
Exchange Rate:	US$1 = 9,664 rupiah £1 = 17,575 rupiah

*(2003) Calculated on Purchasing Power Parity basis
Source: World Bank

INDONESIA'S ISLANDS AND MAJOR CITIES

HISTORY OF INDONESIA UP TO 1945

The spectacular Buddhist monument of Borobudur in Java, built A.D. 750–850.

Little is known about the development of humans on the Indonesian islands. In 1891, a Dutch doctor, Eugene Dubois, discovered fossils of a human ancestor, whom he called Java Man. Java Man is an example of *Homo erectus* (an ancestor of modern humans).

PREHISTORY

Samples found in Indonesia range in age from 40,000 to 1.7 million years. Modern humans (*Homo sapiens*) arrived some 60,000 years ago, so the two species existed at the same time for many thousands of years.

The first settlers in Indonesia are believed to have been descended from Malay (Southeast Asian) and Austro-Melanesian (New Guinean) people. Around 3,000 years ago the Dongson culture, which began in what is now Vietnam and southern China, spread to the archipelago. This marked the beginning of rice cultivation, which has been especially important in Java and Bali.

EARLY KINGDOMS

The religions Hinduism and Buddhism arrived from India around the second century A.D. and spread throughout the main islands. Trade was beginning to flourish between India, China and the Middle East and early kingdoms began to form throughout the archipelago. The Hindu-Buddhist Sriwijaya kingdom on the Sumatran coast grew up around this international trade in the seventh century. In central Java, early kingdoms developed around organized agriculture between the eighth and tenth centuries.

The Majaphit kingdom in the thirteenth century was the first to gain control over much of the archipelago. At this time, more traders from the Middle East were arriving and they started to form larger communities. Islam began to spread along the trade routes and by the sixteenth century it had become the major religion throughout the islands. However, Hinduism remained the dominant religion in some places, such as Bali, and for some people, like the Tengger in east Java.

In 2004, one of the most exciting scientific discoveries of recent years was found on the Indonesian island of Flores. In a limestone cave, scientists found a complete skeleton, along with several bones and teeth from other individuals. The remains were of a new species of hominid (relatives of human beings) called *Homo floresiensis*. These people measured about 1m (3 feet) tall, with a brain one third the size of a modern human's (*Homo sapiens*). Tests on the bones estimated they were 18,000 years old. This means that these people lived at the same time as modern humans for thousands of years. Indonesian legends talk of small peoples living in the forests even today.

Scientists compare the small skull of *Homo floresiensis* with the skull of modern humans.

COLONIALISM

European countries were also expanding trade and their power throughout the world. The Portuguese, looking to dominate the lucrative spice trade in the sixteenth century, were the first Europeans to arrive in Indonesia.

Spices remain important agricultural products in Indonesia today.

However, it was the Dutch, through the United East Indies Company, who established power in the islands and took complete control of the spice trade. In 1799, the Dutch government took direct control of the region from the trading company. It established the Dutch East Indies as part of the Dutch empire, with its capital in Batavia (now Jakarta). Dutch rule continued until the Second World War and the Japanese invasion of Indonesia in 1942.

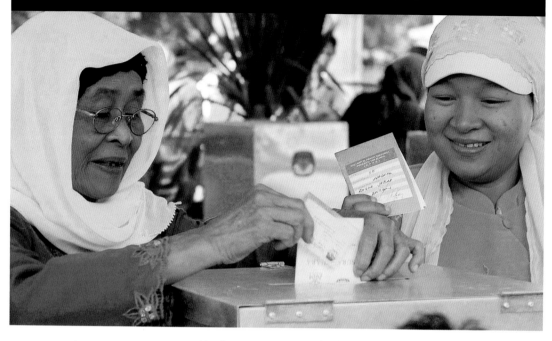

Muslim women vote in the first direct presidential elections in 2004.

By the Second World War, many Indonesians were unhappy with being ruled over by foreign powers and wanted independence. On August 17, 1945, two days after the Japanese surrendered, the Indonesian nationalist movement, led by Sukarno and Muhammad Hatta, declared independence from the Netherlands. The Dutch returned to claim their colony and bitter fighting raged until 1949, despite negotiations led by the United Nations. On December 27, 1949, power was officially handed over, except for Papua, which the Dutch retained until 1963.

INDEPENDENCE AND PRESIDENT SUKARNO

Sukarno became the first president of the new Republic of Indonesia in 1950. Democracy was plagued with political divisions and regional rebellions in this early period. To try and increase political stability, Sukarno introduced a new system of rule called Guided Democracy. Sukarno and the cabinet took more control, limiting the say of parliament and the people. With Sukarno moving closer toward the Indonesian Communist Party (called the PKI) – the third-largest communist party in the world after those of the Soviet Union and China – the military felt they were losing their political power.

SUHARTO – 30 YEARS OF RULE

On September 30, 1965, there was an attempted coup (takeover of power) by dissident officers. General Suharto seized the initiative – he took control of the armed forces and blamed the coup on the PKI. There was a purge of anyone suspected of being a communist. Between 160,000 and 500,000 people are reported to have died in these attacks. Sukarno's political position became very weak and Suharto gradually took power.

The PKI was banned and Suharto became president in 1968.

Suharto set about creating a so-called New Order, where expanding the economy had central importance. Life improved for many people, but corruption was a major problem, with the friends and family of Suharto making huge fortunes. Any challenges to Suharto's authoritarian rule were crushed and he remained president for 30 years. The end of Suharto began with the Asian economic crisis in 1997, made worse by falling oil prices and widespread drought. Pro-democracy demonstrations led by students, rioting over rising prices, and power struggles within the military eventually gave Suharto no option but to resign on May 21, 1998.

POLITICAL REFORM AND DEMOCRACY

Vice President B. J. Habibie replaced Suharto, and he called the first national elections in 1999 – a major move toward political reform after almost four decades of authoritarian rule. Abdurrahman Wahid became president, but parliament impeached him. His successor was Megawati Sukarnoputri – the daughter of former president Sukarno. In September 2004, Susilo Bambang Yudhoyono became the first president to be directly elected by the Indonesian people. He has promised to fight corruption, rejuvenate the economy and tackle separatist conflict.

CASE STUDY
EAST TIMOR

In 1975, East Timor gained independence from the Portuguese. Suharto feared that the success of East Timor's separatists would inspire separatist rebellions in Indonesia. So, in December 1975, Indonesian armed forces invaded the country, and East Timor became a province of Indonesia in 1976. During this period it is estimated between 100,000 and 200,000 East Timorese died from violence or famine.

In 1999, East Timorese were given a referendum on their future and voted for independence. Pro-Indonesian militia began a campaign of terror throughout the region. United Nations (UN) peacekeeping forces arrived to restore order. With UN assistance, East Timor gained independence from Indonesia in May 2002, but the transition has not been easy. Poverty remains high and security is still a concern.

East Timorese celebrate independence in May 2002.

Mount Bromo is highly significant to the Hindu Tengger people of Java.

From white sandy beaches to smoking volcanic craters, and from deep turquoise seas to snow-capped peaks, Indonesia's spectacular landscape is one of contrasts. With hot tropical weather on the coastal plains as well as cool mountain ranges, and subject to flooding and droughts, the climate is equally varied across the wide-ranging islands.

THE LAND OF FIRE

Indonesia forms part of the Pacific Ring of Fire, a zone around the Pacific plate that has more than half of all the volcanoes above sea level in the world. Indonesia has over 400 volcanoes, of which 129 are active. A chain of volcanoes forms the backbone of Sumatra, Java, Bali and Nusa Tenggara. This loops around through the Banda Islands of Maluku into Sulawesi. These volcanoes have been formed by the movement of tectonic plates, which make up the outer surface of Earth.

The volcanoes from Sumatra to Nusa Tenggara have been formed by the Indo-Australian plate moving underneath the Eurasian plate. As one plate moves below the other – a process called subduction – the rock melts. Molten rock called magma is then forced to the surface a few hundred kilometers away, forming volcanoes.

The interaction of the tectonic plates around Sulawesi and Maluku is more complex. While Sulawesi is at the junction of the Indo-Australian and Eurasian plates, the formation of Malaku is a result of the movement of the Philippines, Eurasian and Pacific plates.

Papua has been formed by the collision of the Indo-Australian and Pacific plates, which has forced the ground upward over millions of years. Along with volcanoes – the highest on the island being Trikora (4,750m) – there are also glaciers. Indonesia is one of only three tropical countries in the world that have glaciers. The glacier on Puncak Jaya (or Mount

On August 26, 1883, one of the most famous volcanic eruptions occurred as Krakatau (sometimes called Krakatoa), a volcanic island in the Sunda Strait, exploded. Ash was sent almost 80km up into the atmosphere – plunging everything within a 250km radius into darkness. The explosion destroyed half of the island, throwing nearly 18km^3 of rock into the sky. It formed a 300m-deep crater underneath the ocean. and raised 40m-high tsunami (giant waves). The tsunami traveled rapidly across the oceans, reaching the African island of Madagascar 10 hours later. It is estimated that 36,000 people died and 165 villages were destroyed in the explosion and eruptions, which continued for two days.

Krakatau was a major world event. These drawings showing the volcano before and after the eruption were published in a London newspaper in 1883.

Jaya) – the highest mountain in Indonesia at 5,039m – is in retreat (getting smaller).

There are 65 observatories in Indonesia, monitoring 59 volcanoes. There have been many famous eruptions in Indonesia, such as Krakatau in 1883. Experts believe Sumatra's

Lake Toba, the largest lake in Southeast Asia, occupies the location of a former volcano that blasted itself away 75,000 years ago in an eruption that dwarfed Krakatau's explosion.

Given their destructive power, it is no surprise most volcanoes have mythical and religious significance. Agung in Bali is considered the center of the Balinese universe, while Java's Tengger people make offerings to Mount Bromo for protection.

MAJOR VOLCANOES

▲ Major volcanoes (with eruptions since 1900)

N

Sulu Sea — PHILIPPINES

Aceh — Nantuna Besar — BRUNEI — Celebes Sea — Api Siau (Karangetang) — Ibu — Halmahera — Equator

PACIFIC OCEAN

Strait of Malacca — MALAYSIA — SINGAPORE — Nias — Sumatra

Kalimantan — Maluku

Bangka — INDONESIA — Sulawesi — Buru — Seram — Papua

Belitung — Java Sea — Bandi Api — PAPUA NEW GUINEA

INDIAN OCEAN — Krakatau — Tengger Caldera — Kelud — Batur — Lombok — Nusa Tenggara — Wetar — Banda Sea — Kepulauan Aru — Kepulauan Tanimbar

Java — Merapi — Bali — Tambora — Flores — EAST TIMOR — West Timor — Arafura Sea

Semeru — Agung — Kelimutu — Timor Sea — AUSTRALIA

0 — 800km
0 — 500 miles

ISLANDS AND SEA

Indonesians typically refer to their country as *tanah air kita*, meaning "our earth and water." There is more than four times as much water as land in Indonesia. The total land area is 1,919,440km^2, which is about triple the size of Texas, but the combined expanse of land and sea makes up an area more than twice the size of the entire United States.

Of the 17,508 islands, only 73 are larger than 500km^2 – about double the size of the city of Chicago. Among these are three of the world's six largest islands. Papua is found on the island of New Guinea (sharing it with Papua New Guinea), which is the second-largest island after Greenland. Borneo, in which lies the Indonesian territory of Kalimantan along with Brunei and parts of Malaysia, is third. Sumatra is the sixth-largest island in the world, and the largest completely Indonesian island.

Geologically, Indonesia's islands fall into three groups. First are the islands that lie on the Sunda continental shelf, including Sumatra, Borneo and Java. Next are Papua and the Aru Islands, which lie on the Sahal shelf. Islands found on these shelves are surrounded by seas no deeper than 215m. Finally, Nusa Tenggara, Maluku and Sulawesi lie between the two shelves and have much greater sea depths – in some places more than 5,000m.

COASTAL PLAINS AND CORAL REEFS

The archipelago provides the ideal marine landscape for corals to grow – clear, warm and shallow water – and consequently there is a vast collection of coral reefs. Freshwater is harmful for corals, so they are found away from the mouths of rivers, but around these river estuaries and sheltered coastal plains are some of the world's most unspoiled mangrove swamps.

Many of the mountainous islands have expansive coastal plains, but some of the islands of Maluku, such as Halmahera, Seram and Buru, have steep sides rising up from the water's edge. There are very few beaches here, just rugged shorelines. Many of the smaller islands remain uninhabited, as they are simply little islands of rock, with no potential for agriculture or settlement.

THE JAVA TRENCH

About 300km off the coast of Sumatra and Java is a deep ocean trench known as the Java Trench (sometimes called the Java Deep Trench or the Sunda Trench). It runs for more than 2,600km in the Indian Ocean and can reach depths of around 7,500m. It is where the Indo-Australian tectonic plate gradually moves underneath the Eurasian plate. The edge of the Eurasian plate is much steeper than the Indo-Australian plate, which is being subducted.

Indonesia's marine environments, such as this coral reef off Bunaken Island, Sulawesi, are some of the most important in the world.

SIZE OF MAJOR ISLANDS

New Guinea	800,311km^2 (Indonesian territory of Papua 421,981km^2)
Borneo	755,000km^2 (Indonesian territory of Kalimantan 539,460km^2)
Sumatra	473, 606km^2
Sulawesi	189,216km^2
Java	125, 622km^2
Timor	30,777km^2 (Indonesian territory of West Timor 16,510km^2)
Bali	5,561km^2

LANDSCAPE FEATURES

THE LAKES OF KELIMUTU

Near the 1,640m summit of the Kelimutu volcano three spectacular lakes can be found. The three crater lakes have different, and changing, colors. At present, the lakes are turquoise, dark brown and black. In recent years they have been blue, dark red and black. In the 1960s the colors were again different – blue, a murky red and a milky brown. It is believed the minerals from volcanic rocks cause the different water colors.

Kelimutu crater lakes on the island of Flores.

In the rainy season especially, sudden heavy downpours can cause local flooding.

CLIMATE

Indonesia has a tropical climate, which means it is warm and humid. The relative humidity is usually between 70 and 90 percent. This can be uncomfortably sticky and explains why many Indonesians prefer to socialize in the cooler evenings. There are two main seasons, the wet – or rainy – and the dry. The wet season typically occurs between October and March. There are tropical downpours, usually in the afternoons, when a lot of rain falls in a short time. The dry season is between April and September, when temperatures are a little warmer.

Maluku is the exception to the general seasonal trends in Indonesia. In central and southern Maluku the dry season is between October and March, when the temperature averages 30°C (86°F). The wet monsoon lasts from May until August, and the temperature falls slightly to 23°C (73°F). However, in north Maluku the rainy season is from December to March, much like the rest of Indonesia.

There is great variation both between islands and within different locations on the same island. The highlands in west Java average 4,000mm of rain a year, while on the northeast coast of Java rainfall measures only 900mm. The town of Bogor is one of the wettest places in Indonesia, with heavy rain around 322 days a year. This is over twice as many days as the capital Jakarta, which is only 60km north of Bogor. The island group of Nusa Tenggara is very dry and this is reflected in its habitats – savannah rather than the rain forests of wetter areas. The closer an island group is to Australia, the longer its dry season tends to be, with droughts a common problem. But the same islands also face flooding in the rainy season because the ground cannot absorb the water fast enough.

The temperature in Indonesia varies according to the height above sea level. At low altitudes, on the coastal plains, the

PRECIPITATION

Rainfall per year (mm)

less than 600	2,000–2,800
600–1,000	2,800–4,000
1,000–1,400	4,000–5,600
1,400–2,000	

N

temperature averages 28°C (82°F). Inland, and at slightly higher elevations, the temperature averages a few degrees less – at 26°C (79°F). In the higher mountain regions, temperatures begin to fall further (unless you are standing on top of an active volcano!).

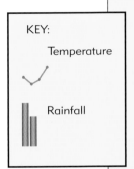

KEY:

Temperature

Rainfall

CASE STUDY
THE PALU VALLEY

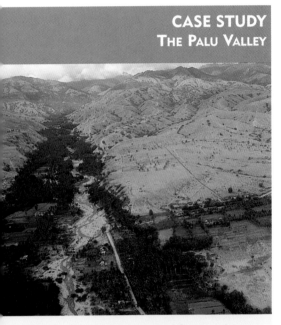

The dry Palu Valley in central Sulawesi has hot days and cooler nights.

It is reported that the Palu Valley in Sulawesi is the driest place in Indonesia, with less than 500mm of rain a year. It is interesting because Palu lies only a few kilometers away from lush tropical rain forest. The winds in Sulawesi typically blow from the west, the northwest or the southeast. The valley runs from north to south. The orientation of the mountain range relative to the air circulation causes the rain clouds that form to deposit the water on the windward side. On the other side of the mountain – called the leeward side – very little rain falls. The Palu Valley is on the leeward side and remains very dry.

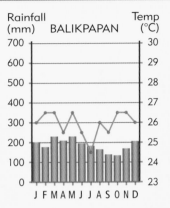

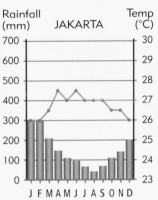

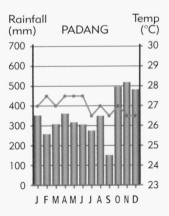

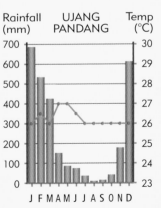

Fixing a pipe on a tanker so oil can be shipped around the world.

Indonesia's economy was heavily dependent on the production of oil and gas until the mid-1980s, when the government began to develop other industries and manufacturing expanded. The population provided a large cheap workforce, which made Indonesian products very competitive around the world.

In the 1990s, there was a major increase in international investment. Foreign companies were arriving in Indonesia, wanting to take advantage of the large labor force and the country's ideal location for distributing products around the world. This expansion led to an increase of gross domestic product (GDP) by about 8 percent per year in the 1990s.

THE 1997 ECONOMIC CRISIS

In July 1997, the World Bank forecast a great future for the Indonesian economy. This was soon to change as an economic crisis – starting in Thailand, then moving on to Malaysia and Indonesia – hit Southeast Asia. In July 1997 US$1 was worth 2,600 rupiah. Throughout the economic crisis the value of the currency rapidly declined. It eventually stabilized in 1998 – at around 10,000 rupiah to US$1. At its lowest point, one dollar could buy 17,000 rupiah. This was a disaster for the economy. International companies quickly withdrew billions of dollars to save their

investments. Local companies were in trouble. Many had borrowed money from overseas and had to pay it back in US dollars – yet they earned rupiah, which now was worth much less. Many Indonesians lost their businesses and the number of people living below the poverty line increased.

THE ECONOMY TODAY

Following the crisis, the Indonesian economy shrank. Today, it is growing again, but at a much slower rate than in the 1990s. The amount of money the government owes from borrowing, called the national debt, is US$130.8 billion. The major industries in Indonesia today are the manufacturing of paper and pulp, cement, and fertilizers; the extraction of basic metals; power generation; telecommunications; and transport. The country is a major exporter of textiles, garments and shoes, oil and gas, electrical goods, and wood products. Indonesia's main imports are chemicals and pharmaceuticals, cotton yarns and fabrics used in the textile industry, motor vehicles, and industrial

MAJOR TRADING PARTNERS (% OF VALUE), 2003

EXPORTS

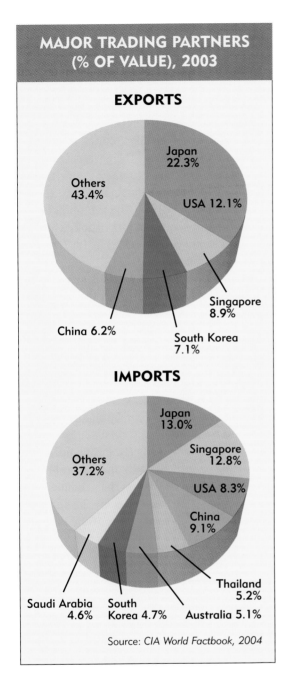

Japan 22.3%
USA 12.1%
Others 43.4%
Singapore 8.9%
South Korea 7.1%
China 6.2%

IMPORTS

Japan 13.0%
Singapore 12.8%
USA 8.3%
China 9.1%
Others 37.2%
Thailand 5.2%
Australia 5.1%
South Korea 4.7%
Saudi Arabia 4.6%

Source: *CIA World Factbook, 2004*

GNI PER CAPITA (US$)

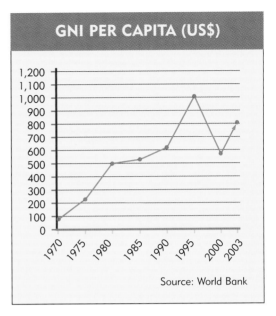

Source: World Bank

ELECTRICITY PRODUCTION BY SOURCE

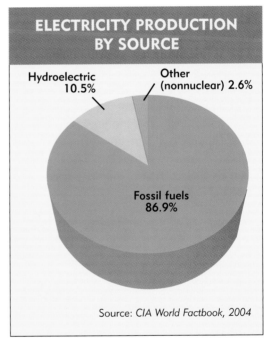

Hydroelectric 10.5%
Other (nonnuclear) 2.6%
Fossil fuels 86.9%

Source: *CIA World Factbook, 2004*

machinery. The service industries – including tourism, banking, health, and education – are also growing.

OIL AND GAS

Indonesia is among the top ten producers of natural gas in the world, having reserves of 2.549 trillion cubic meters. Of the 69 billion cubic meters produced each year, 32.8 billion cubic meters are exported. Indonesia is the world's biggest producer of liquefied natural gas (LNG). This is natural gas that has been converted into a liquid form, reducing its volume by 600 times so it is easier to transport overseas. At the end of its journey, LNG is returned to its natural gaseous state by exposure to heat. Indonesia is also a major oil producer – averaging 1.2 million barrels per day. In 1990, gas and oil accounted for 43.1 percent of export earnings, but this fell to 21.1 percent in 2003 as the manufacturing and service sectors expanded.

MINING

Indonesia has a wealth of mining potential. Large areas of the archipelago have not been surveyed yet, so the full possibilities are not known. However, the sector is in crisis. In 1999, in a move to safeguard the environment, the government banned open-pit mining in protected forested areas. Many large companies had already signed contracts with the government to develop projects in these areas. The resulting uncertainty has drastically reduced investment in mining since 1999. To try and boost the sector, in May 2004 the government permitted 13 companies with operations in place to continue and authorized nine more with exploration contracts to restart work.

Coal is one of the few growth mining industries in Indonesia. In 2003, Indonesia extracted 109.3 million tonnes, an increase of 6.3 million tonnes from 2002. Of this, 70 percent is exported. Indonesia has the world's largest coal mine in northeast Kalimantan, run by Kaltim Prima Coal (KPC). The mine makes US$450 million per year from coal exports.

Indonesia is also a leading supplier of tin, with estimated deposits of 1 million tonnes. Nickel is another metallic element in abundance – 4.4 million tonnes were mined in 2003.

Indonesia has 500 million tonnes of bauxite (aluminum ore) reserves. The government and the Japanese Overseas Economic Cooperation Fund jointly funded an aluminum smelting plant in north Sumatra in 1985. The plant processes the bauxite for aluminum production, which increased from 808,749 tonnes in 1997, to 1.3 million tonnes in 2003.

Gold and silver are two precious metals mined in Indonesia. From 1983 to 2001 the production of gold increased by over 70 times, from 2,340kg to 166,100kg. In the same period, silver increased almost 10 times. Since 2001, the amount of both silver and gold produced has declined slightly. Part of the reason for this is local opposition to mines. In 2003, a gold mine in Halmahera, Maluku – run by an Australian company, Gold Crest – was occupied by demonstrators who disrupted mining operations. Many local people complain that the profits of mining are not put back into their communities. Instead, they often face relocation, loss of land and pollution problems created by the mines.

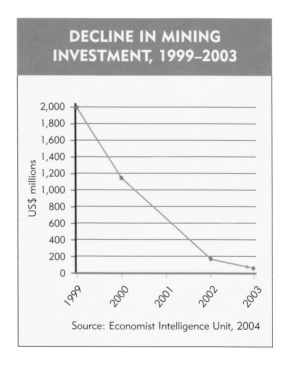

Environmental groups believe that open-pit mining in protected forest areas will have devastating consequences.

DECLINE IN MINING INVESTMENT, 1999–2003

US$ millions

Source: Economist Intelligence Unit, 2004

The Grasberg open-pit mine in Papua is the second-largest copper mine and the largest gold mine in the world. From copper alone, the mine is estimated to make US$1 million a day. It is run by Freeport Indonesia, part of the US-owned Freeport McMoRan company. It employs 18,000 people, but only about 30 percent are Papuan – the rest come from other parts of Indonesia or are foreign workers. Although the company spends money on community development, many feel this is inadequate compensation for the relocation of villages caused by the mine.

Freeport McMoRan admitted to paying the Indonesian armed forces US$5.6 million in 2002 for security services. The company and the Indonesian armed forces have been criticized for alleged brutality against protestors. Protests have focused on the destruction of over 30,000 hectares of rain forest and damage to rivers. Local indigenous groups claim to have lost ancestral lands.

The Grasberg mine remains controversial for its destruction of forest and ancestral lands.

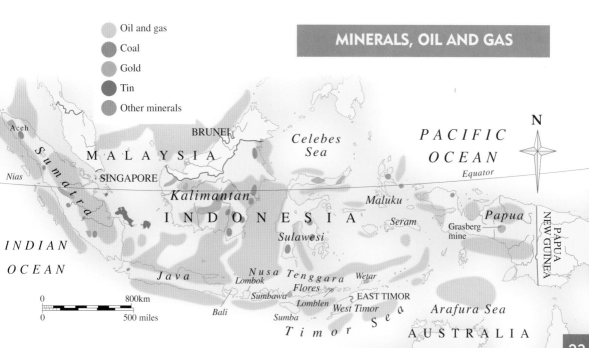

MINERALS, OIL AND GAS

- Oil and gas
- Coal
- Gold
- Tin
- Other minerals

Aceh

Nias

Sumatra

BRUNEI

MALAYSIA

SINGAPORE

Celebes Sea

PACIFIC OCEAN

Equator

Kalimantan

INDONESIA

Maluku

Seram

Papua

Grasberg mine

PAPUA NEW GUINEA

Sulawesi

N

INDIAN OCEAN

Java

Lombok

Nusa Tenggara

Flores

Wetar

Sumbawa

Lomblen

West Timor

EAST TIMOR

Bali

Sumba

Arafura Sea

Timor Sea

AUSTRALIA

0   800km
0   500 miles

AGRICULTURE

The largest share of Indonesia's labor force – 45 percent – works in agriculture. Although its share in the country's GDP has been declining as manufacturing and service industries have expanded, the agricultural sector has still grown. Arable land increased from 9.9 percent of all land in 1980 to 11.3 percent in 2001. Similarly, permanent cropland rose in the same period, from 4.4 to 7.2 percent.

Indonesia is famous for rice production, especially the irrigated rice terraces of Java and Bali. It is the third-largest producer of rice in the world. In 1985, the country was self-sufficient – producing enough rice for the population to eat. With transmigration (see page 34), the popularity of rice has spread to islands where historically other foods, like cassava, formed the staple crop. With population growth as well, Indonesia has needed to import rice since 1985. However, with increasing rice cultivation, the

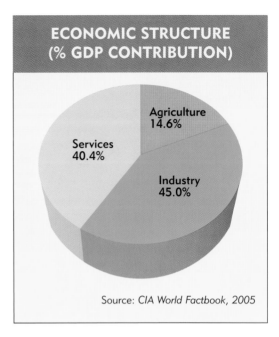

ECONOMIC STRUCTURE (% GDP CONTRIBUTION)

Agriculture 14.6%
Services 40.4%
Industry 45.0%

Source: *CIA World Factbook, 2005*

government announced Indonesia was again self-sufficient in rice at the end of 2004.

Spices have been historically important to the islands. During the colonial period, mace (the outer covering of nutmeg, used as a spice) was more expensive than its weight in gold. Although the spice trade is not as important as it once was, it still earns Indonesia over US$186 million a year. It is the largest producer of nutmeg and second only to India in pepper production.

The cultivation of coffee and cocoa is increasing as plantations expand. Indonesia is the largest producer of the robusta coffee bean, earning US$218.8 million in 2002, and the second-largest cocoa producer behind Côte d'Ivoire. Rubber, another plantation crop, earns Indonesia around US$1.5 billion a year.

Oil-palm cultivation is a rapidly expanding agricultural endeavor. In 2002, almost 10 million tonnes of crude palm oil were produced on large plantations, employing some 2 million people.

LEFT: Nutmeg pickers on the Banda Islands. When the fruit is ripe it splits, revealing the nutmeg.

Rice cultivation requires vast amounts of water. For centuries, the terrace rice farmers of Bali have arranged access to water at local water temples. The farmers make offerings to the gods and goddesses, and the water priests bless the crop. The water priests are responsible for making sure each farmer has a fair share of the water, and they sort out all disputes.

In the 1970s, the Indonesian government wanted to modernize agricultural production. Farmers were encouraged to grow more rice by using new fertilizers and pesticides. The water priests no longer controlled the allocation of water. More water was used in the new system, and at first there was an increase in rice yields. This did not last – shortages of water became a problem, and the rice crop became infested by pests.

The rice farmers wanted to go back to the traditional system. The government opposed this, because the system of water allocation was not scientifically proven. In 1987, an American scientist developed a computer model of the Balinese agricultural system that demonstrated the ecological success of water sharing by the priests. Faced with this scientific explanation the government backed down, and the water priests are again in control.

The major Balinese water temple of Ulun Danu, which controls the vast water resources of Lake Batur for rice farmers.

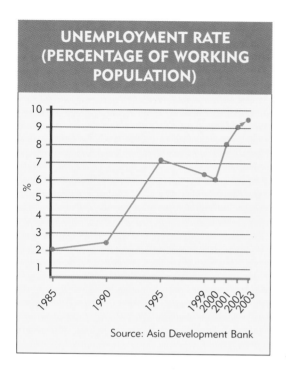

UNEMPLOYMENT RATE (PERCENTAGE OF WORKING POPULATION)

%

Source: Asia Development Bank

FISHERIES

The seas surrounding Indonesia are a major source of income for the country. In 2002, exported shrimp brought more than US$840 million into the country. Fish and other marine products, excluding shrimp, were worth US$378 million in the same year. These figures have the potential to be higher, but illegal fishing in Indonesian waters is reducing the legal catch. Though the government is now cracking down on illegal boats, they still reduce revenue by up to US$1 billion and cause a decline in the fish stocks.

MANUFACTURING

FOREST PRODUCTS

The vast forests of Indonesia are a valuable natural resource and have made the country the largest exporter of forest products in

Hardwoods arrive in Jakarta from Kalimantan for use in the construction industry.

Changes in world trade threaten many jobs in the textile industry.

Southeast Asia. Revenue from forest products has fallen since the economic crisis, however, because construction demand declined and logging quotas were reduced to stop the overexploitation of the forests. But there is a vast illegal trade of logging and smuggling, estimated to be worth US$7.2 billion – compared with official trade of around US$3.2 billion a year.

Plywood production, based in Kalimantan (along with pulp and paper manufacturing), has been criticized for exceeding logging quotas. By the end of 1999, there were 88 paper mills with a capacity to produce 10.7 million tonnes of paper each year. To reach these maximum levels 25 million cubic meters of timber were required. But only 3.5 million cubic meters were available to the industry, so much of the shortfall was made up of illegally logged trees.

TEXTILES

The textile, garment and footwear industry provides the second-largest income from overseas exports after oil and gas, worth around US$10 billion per year. Cotton is imported for making garments, but with its abundance of petrochemicals (from oil and gas) Indonesia is able to produce nylon, polyester and other synthetic fabrics.

The textile industry – the largest employer of women in the manufacturing sector – is under serious threat. In 2002, 242 companies went bankrupt. Many companies could not compete with lower labor costs in countries such as Vietnam and Cambodia. The situation may worsen. For years, US and European import quotas protected Indonesia's textile industry. These quotas disappeared in 2005, and Indonesia may not be able to compete with large-scale producers like India and China that have cheaper labor.

CEMENT AND OTHER PRODUCTS

The production of cement is an important industry in Indonesia, supplying both the domestic and international markets. During the economic boom years of the 1980s and early 1990s, the construction (building) industry expanded, increasing the need for cement production. In 2001, 8 million tonnes was exported, with a value of US$161 million. In 2002, cement exports fell as the construction industry in Indonesia began to grow – consequently requiring more cement for domestic use.

Machinery and electrical appliances provide the third-largest earnings from exports. This reached an all-time high of US$10.3 billion in 2000, declining to US$8.6 billion in 2001.

27

TOURISM

Tourism is an expanding service industry in Indonesia. In 1993, just over 3.4 million people visited Indonesia, and tourism reached a peak of almost 5.2 million in 1997. Following the riots and violence in May 1998 (see pages 12–13), fewer tourists visited the country, but from 1999 to 2002, tourist numbers rose again. Australians are the most frequent tourists to the islands, making up 27 percent of international visitors.

The end of 2002 was the beginning of a troubled year for tourism in Indonesia. After a popular tourist area in Bali was bombed in October, the fear of terrorism reduced the numbers arriving. This was followed by the outbreak of SARS (severe acute respiratory syndrome), which kept large numbers of

CASE STUDY
THE BALI BOMBINGS

On October 12, 2002, a bomb exploded in the popular tourist destination of Kuta on Bali. The bomb blasted through clubs and bars, injuring well over 300 people and killing 202. People of 23 different nationalities died in the bomb blast, most of them Indonesian and Australian. Another bomb also exploded near the US consulate in Sanur, near Kuta, without causing injury or death.

The effect on tourism was immediate – governments around the world issued warnings against traveling to Indonesia in case of further attacks. The monthly numbers of tourists arriving fell dramatically – from 150,747 in September to 31,498 in November. The attacks were linked to an Islamic extremist organization called Jemaah Islamiah. In August 2003, four suspects were sentenced for the bombings. Three were given the death penalty.

Police investigate the bombing of a nightclub in Kuta in October 2002.

Legend:
— Main road
······ Railroad
✈ International airport

visitors away from the whole of Southeast Asia and China. Tourist-related businesses suffered, and unemployment increased. By early 2004 tourist numbers were starting to grow, but a second Bali bombing in October 2005 again discouraged potential visitors.

Indonesia is a very popular place to go snorkeling and scuba diving, but these activities can damage the marine habitat. The growth of ecotourism should help to encourage protection of the environment and provide a good source of income for local communities. The diversity of Indonesian peoples and their rich traditions provide an opportunity to expand cultural tourism. Cultural tourism allows visitors to see, learn and appreciate different ideas and ways of living.

TRANSPORTATION AND COMMUNICATIONS

The Strait of Malacca, which lies between Malaysia and Indonesia, receives one quarter of all maritime trade in the world. Some 50,000 ships a year pass through the channel, which is only 1.5 nautical miles wide at its narrowest point. In 2003, 27 percent of the world's illegal attacks on ships occurred here, posing a potential environmental hazard since many vessels using the strait are taking oil to Japan, China and South Korea.

Ferries and other boats link the islands in the archipelago. River travel in Indonesia is not widespread because most rivers are too narrow or too shallow for larger boats. Kalimantan, with its extensive water networks, is the exception, and boats are used to access the more remote areas. Road building is increasing throughout the archipelago – Indonesia has more than 340,000km of highways – though future road-building plans threaten to pass through important ecological areas.

Indonesia is famous for its beaches and surfing, attracting people from all over the world.

A busy street scene in Bandung, central Java. Indonesia's large population contains many ethnic groups.

Indonesia is a hugely diverse nation with many different peoples and cultures. This is summed up well by its national motto – *bhinneka tunggal ika* – meaning "unity in diversity" or "they are many, they are one." This diversity does cause pressures at times, but for the most part, Indonesians manage to live peacefully together.

ETHNIC DIVERSITY

There are over 300 different ethnic groups in Indonesia, speaking over 350 different languages. The languages can be divided into two main groups – Malay and Papuan. The Malay languages (over 200) are related to those on mainland Southeast Asia and originate from the Malay ancestors who first spread through the islands from west to east. The 150 Papuan languages reflect the people first arriving in the east of the archipelago. The island of New Guinea (Papua of Indonesia and the separate country of Papua New Guinea) accounts for 15 percent of all the known languages in the world.

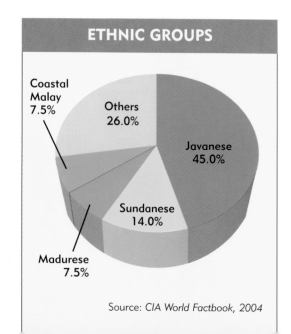

ETHNIC GROUPS

Coastal Malay 7.5%
Others 26.0%
Javanese 45.0%
Sundanese 14.0%
Madurese 7.5%

Source: *CIA World Factbook*, 2004

FUNERAL CEREMONIES OF THE TORAJA

The Toraja on Sulawesi have elaborate funeral ceremonies called the *tomate* – if not carried out, the soul of the deceased will bring misfortune to the family. The first funeral is immediately after the death. The body is preserved and remains in the house while arrangements are made for the grand second funeral. This can take months, depending on the time of the year, as people wait for the dry season. The ceremony involves animal sacrifices, dancing, singing and eating and can last several days.

Some ethnic groups, like the Badui and the Kubu, remained isolated from the outside world as trade began to develop. Others, like the Balinese and Javanese, have had a long history of contact with outsiders. Many groups periodically moved around territories as they cultivated new areas for food and allowed old areas to regenerate, a practice known as swidden agriculture. The changing economy means many ethnic groups have lost their ancestral lands and have had to settle in permanent communities. The Bajo people traditionally lived on the seas, traveling between Indonesia, Malaysia and the Philippines. The Bajo still dive for sea cucumbers, pearls and other sea products, but they also have settled communities on the mainland.

The Javanese make up the largest ethnic group in Indonesia (45 percent), but Bahasa Indonesian became the national language, not Javanese. This was important for Indonesia when it gained independence, because it gave the crucial message that all the islands, not just Java, were of equal importance.

The Chinese have been trading on the Indonesian islands for centuries. In the seventeenth century, only men were allowed to migrate from China. Some of these Chinese men settled on the islands and married local women. Children with a Chinese father and Indonesian mother were known as Chinese Peranakans. When they grew up, they tended to marry other Chinese Peranakans, so a new ethnic group was formed. Over the generations, Bahasa Indonesian has become their first language, with Chinese second. Unlike similar groups in Malaysia (the Babas) – and in the Philippines (Mestizos) – the Peranakans have remained a distinct group within Indonesia, accounting for almost 3 percent of the population.

Traditional Peranakan dress worn during a festival following the Chinese New Year.

POPULATION TRENDS

Indonesia has the world's fourth-largest population behind China, India and the United States. Since the 1950s, the population has nearly tripled, from just over 79.5 million people to almost 212 million in 2000.

Under President Sukarno's leadership, families were encouraged to have as many children as possible. This was part of a plan to provide a large workforce that would enable Indonesian industry to compete with the rest of the world, bringing money and development to the country. The expansion was aimed at increasing the number of people and industries on those islands that had smaller populations.

When Suharto came to power the population program was reversed. People were encouraged to plan the size of their families – to help reduce the growth in the population. This was focused especially in areas with high populations, such as Java and Bali. It was reported that 80 percent of people using the state-provided family planning services were from poorer families, who traditionally tended to have larger families. Many people, especially in Java, believe the saying *dua anak cukup*, which means "two children are enough."

The sizes of families continue to be larger in areas with strong Muslim communities. Parents in rural areas also often have more children than those in urban areas. This acts as "insurance" for the parents in old age, making sure someone is there to look after them and their land. Overall, in Indonesia there has been a decline in the birth rate in recent years; this means that fewer people are being born each year. However, more people are being born than the number of people dying, so the population is still increasing. It is estimated that over the next 20 years, Indonesia's population will increase on average by about 2 million a year.

The size of families is declining, especially within major urban areas.

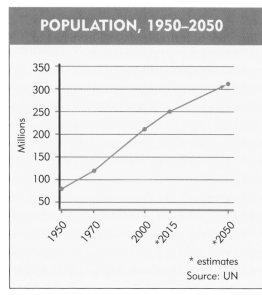

POPULATION, 1950–2050

* estimates
Source: UN

Children in a mangrove fishing village, Kalimantan.

POPULATION STRUCTURE

Every 10 years the government takes a census, which includes a great deal of information about the population. This was last carried out in 2000. The structure of the population is one such piece of information. There are only slightly more men in Indonesia than women. Also, 30 percent of the population was under the age of 15, and more than half was under the age of 25. This is very different from the US population structure, in which only 13.5 percent of the population is under age 15 and 35 percent under age 25.

The large percentage of young people in Indonesia means the government is under pressure to provide enough social and welfare services – such as education and immunization programs. With the declining birth rates and increasing life expectancy, the structure will have changed by the next census in 2010. There will be a smaller percentage of young people in the population. In the next decade unemployment could be a major problem. More jobs will need to be created to meet the growing population reaching working age, or unemployment and poverty will increase.

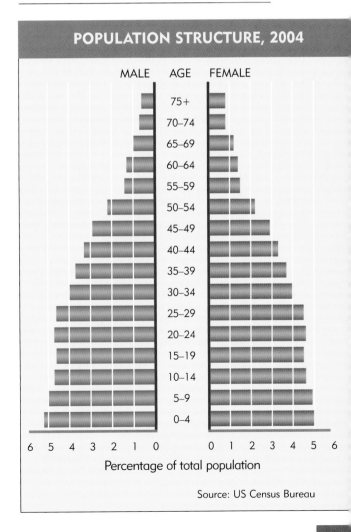

POPULATION STRUCTURE, 2004

MALE   AGE   FEMALE

| 75+ |
| 70–74 |
| 65–69 |
| 60–64 |
| 55–59 |
| 50–54 |
| 45–49 |
| 40–44 |
| 35–39 |
| 30–34 |
| 25–29 |
| 20–24 |
| 15–19 |
| 10–14 |
| 5–9 |
| 0–4 |

6 5 4 3 2 1 0   0 1 2 3 4 5 6

Percentage of total population

Source: US Census Bureau

In 1971, almost 4.6 million people lived in Jakarta; in 2000, it was nearly 8.4 million.

URBANIZATION AND MIGRATION

POPULATION DISTRIBUTION

The average population density of Indonesia is 109 people per square kilometer. However, the population is very unevenly distributed across the archipelago. Papua has the lowest population density, only 6 people per square kilometer, compared with Jakarta, which has the highest at 12,635 people per square kilometer. The majority of the population – 59 percent – live on the island of Java, which is less than 7 percent of the total land area of Indonesia. This pressure on the land has prompted the state to redistribute the population from the densely settled areas of Java and Bali to other islands.

TRANSMIGRASI – MOVING TO THE OUTER ISLANDS

The transmigration – *transmigrasi* in Bahasa Indonesian – was started by the Dutch in 1905. It was a process of moving people away from the densely populated islands of Java and Bali to the outer islands. The Dutch moved 650,000 people, mainly from Java to Sumatra. The Indonesian government continued this policy after independence and expanded it with the support of the World

Bank in 1974, believing this would diversify and strengthen the economy. Sumatra continued to be the major destination in the 1970s, but this changed to Papua (then called Irian Jaya) and Kalimantan in the 1980s. Between 1905 and 1999, 6.2 million people were moved; 3.2 million of these moved between 1984 and 1989. About two thirds of the transmigrants have been landless peasants from rural areas.

Environmental and social problems are associated with the transmigration policy. Forests have been cleared to create new farmland, which has often been poorly used as settlers have attempted to grow unsuitable crops. Tensions have grown in some communities over the ownership and use of land (see pages 36–37). In addition, the policy has been criticized for its expense – and because it has not actually reduced the population density of Java and Bali.

URBANIZATION

In the last 50 years the Indonesian population has undergone a major shift in where they live. In the 1950s, only 12 percent of the population lived in towns and cities; now this

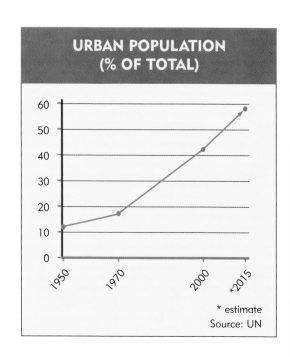

URBAN POPULATION (% OF TOTAL)

* estimate
Source: UN

figure is nearly 50 percent. With the increase in manufacturing and service industries, more and more people are attracted to the cities and towns to find paid employment. Following the economic and political crisis of 1997–98, large numbers of people left the major cities. Many of the Chinese left Indonesia, because they faced violence and their businesses were looted or destroyed. Other people left to go back to rural areas. They thought they would be able to at least grow some of their own food, which was becoming too expensive for many of the poorer people in the cities. As the economy begins to grow again it is likely more people will start heading back to urban areas. Unfortunately, many people find that the cities do not offer them all the opportunities they had hoped for: They cannot find employment; they have no land to grow their own food; and they have to live in cramped conditions.

POPULATION DENSITIES (PEOPLE PER km^2)

Jakarta	12,635
Java (excluding Jakarta)	927
Bali	559
Nusa Tenggara	141
Sumatra	92
Sulawesi	82
Kalimantan	30
Maluku	25
Papua	6

Source: Central Bureau of Statistics, Indonesian Census, 2000

More Indonesians are moving away from the rural areas in search of better prospects.

CONFLICT AND RECONCILIATION

Members of the Free Aceh Movement, who are fighting for independence from Indonesia.

Many people view Indonesia as a violent society. Indeed, the size and diversity of the population do create some tensions, which have caused violent outbursts. Often, religion is blamed for conflict. In some cases, religion does play a part, but in many situations it is perhaps simply the easiest distinction for the media to make between the two sides. Conflicts arise in Indonesia for a wide range of social, cultural, political and economic reasons. However, most Indonesians live peacefully and have shown the ability to reconcile their differences in many situations.

There are some groups, such as the Free Aceh Movement and the Free Papua Movement, that want to gain independence from Indonesia. They are known as separatist groups and have been fighting with the government since the 1970s. Attempts at peace have been made, but no long-term solutions have yet been found. There are many reasons why these groups want independence. One economic reason is to have control of the natural resources in a region, so that any profits made are put back into the local communities.

The transmigration policy of the Indonesian government has also caused conflict between communities. Problems arise from the loss of land and the loss of local control. Small indigenous communities can quickly become outnumbered, leading to a loss of self-identity and culture – and this can create tensions.

CASE STUDY
TRANSMIGRASI PRESSURES IN KALIMANTAN

Conflict between the Dayaks of Kalimantan and ethnic Madurese broke out in 1997. Madurese transmigrants began arriving in Kalimantan in the 1950s. In the port town of Sampit in 2001, it is estimated between 270 and 500 Madurese, including children, were killed by groups of Dayaks. Dayaks were unhappy with the domination of the Madurese in their homeland. The population in Sampit at that time was 60 percent Madurese. About 30,000 ethnic Madurese, even those born on Kalimantan, entered refugee camps or fled the island to Java and Madura. This placed a lot of pressure on both the locations the refugees fled to and the refugees themselves, who now need to find jobs and start new lives.

A young Dayak in front of a burning Madurese house near Sampit in the 2001 violence.

Indonesia has suffered terrorist attacks in recent years, including the Bali bombings in 2002 and 2005 and the car bombs outside the Marriott Hotel in 2003 and the Australian embassy in 2004. These attacks have been linked to Islamic extremist groups. It is very important to remember, however, that the vast majority of Indonesians do not support religious or political extremism of any sort. Extremists number only in the hundreds, at most thousands, in a population of nearly 212 million people.

CASE STUDY
RECONCILIATION IN POSO, SULAWESI

Fighting began in Poso, in Sulawesi, in 1998 over local politics, transmigration pressures and the forced reallocation of land. It divided communities that previously had lived happily together along religious lines. Christians and Muslims clashed, burning down buildings and killing an estimated 2,000 people between 1999 and 2002. Tens of thousands of people fled their homes. In December 2001, the Malino Peace Accord was signed by all sides involved. Road blocks have been removed and people are tentatively going back to areas where they once lived. Reconciliation meetings, counseling, and interfaith volleyball games are arranged by local communities in association with the government, United Nations agencies and nongovernmental organizations (NGOs). Tension is still high, but people are making a strong effort to reconcile differences and live together again peacefully.

Rich and poor: unequal neighbors in Jakarta.

There are major differences in the daily lives of people in Indonesia. Culture, religion, location and wealth are all major factors. Poverty is widespread, with a growing gap between the richest and poorest. Basic services are lacking in rural areas, and many who move to the cities for paid employment often find themselves living in the cramped kampongs (densely packed districts, housing mainly poor people).

Poverty is still a major concern in Indonesia. In 2002, more than half the population lived on the equivalent of less than US$2 a day. Many more live near the poverty line and are called the marginal poor. These people are very vulnerable to entering poverty. A family illness, the loss of a job, or having to look after another relative can send these people falling well below the poverty line. The government is making efforts to reduce the number of people in poverty, but this is made more difficult by rising unemployment.

The differences between the rich and poor are very evident in Indonesia. Kampongs often lie between rich neighborhoods. For example, in the middle of Jakarta, a 2-meter fence separates the five-star international Shangri-La Hotel from the Karet Tensin kampong. Kampongs are often located next to polluted canals and streams, lacking basic services. Without sanitation and clean water these places suffer high rates of waterborne diseases. The poor quality of the housing is even more evident when compared with the rich neighborhoods, where the houses are luxurious by any standards. Some of these wealthy communities have secure gates at the entrances to stop unwanted people from coming in. The city authorities have begun a Kampong Improvement Program to provide better services to the people of the deprived areas.

Access to basic services is increasing in Indonesia. In 1990, only 71 percent of people overall had access to an improved water source; this grew to 78 percent in 2000. Access to improved sanitation still remains low, only increasing from 47 percent in 1990 to 55 percent in 2000. Access to basic services is even lower in rural areas. Only 69 percent of rural inhabitants, compared with 90 percent of urban dwellers, had access to an improved water source.

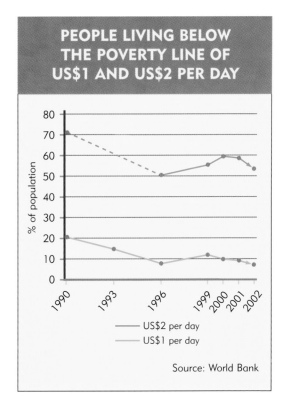

PEOPLE LIVING BELOW THE POVERTY LINE OF US$1 AND US$2 PER DAY

US$2 per day
US$1 per day

Source: World Bank

CASE STUDY
WATER IN THE MARUNDA KAMPONG

Marunda is a kampong in Jakarta that houses about 20,000 people. It was forced to relocate in 1984 to the northeast of the city as the original area began to be developed. The move left Marunda without a source of water or sanitation, and this created many health problems for the community. As part of the Kampong Improvement Program, the city authorities, along with the British company Thames Water, began a $113,000 project to improve access to water and sanitation. The project began in 1999 and worked with 2,000 local people. By 2000, municipal water had been connected directly to 1,600 homes and 12,000 people had access to clean water.

These workers are digging a trench for a new water pipe, as part of the Kampong Improvement Program in Marunda, Jakarta.

HEALTH

Indonesia has been successful in lowering the mortality rate of children under five: The 2001 rate is just one fifth that of 1960. Also, life expectancy has increased by 25 years – from 41 in 1960 to 66 in 2001. This has been as a result of better sanitation and access to clean water, improved diets, national vaccination programs and improved health care. However,

LIFE EXPECTANCY AT BIRTH

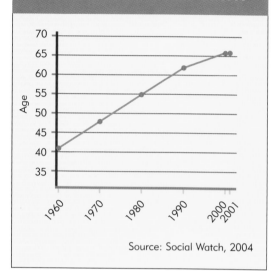

Source: Social Watch, 2004

UNDER-FIVE MORTALITY RATE (DEATHS PER 1,000 BIRTHS)

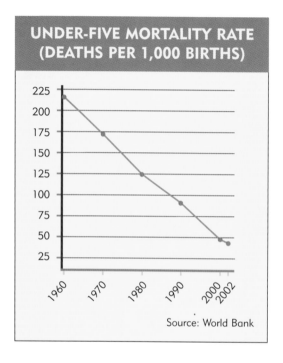

Source: World Bank

there is still a long way to go to match the levels of many developed nations. Only 55.8 percent of mothers giving birth have a skilled health worker present, and they are more than 13 times as likely to die while having their baby as women in the United States. Access to medical facilities and staff is much easier in urban than rural areas.

Indonesia has many health problems it is trying to tackle, such as malaria and tuberculosis. In 2003, the health authorities responded quickly to the outbreak of SARS

KRETEK CIGARETTES

Smoking is a popular habit for Indonesian men: 59 percent of men and only 4 percent of women smoke. Indonesian cigarettes are not simply tobacco. Instead, the tobacco is mixed with cloves and usually wrapped in corn husks to make kretek cigarettes. These are much higher in nicotine and tar than ordinary cigarettes, so the health risks are greater.

Women hand-rolling kretek cigarettes.

The challenge is to enable these primary school children to complete their full education.

(severe acute respiratory syndrome) to minimize the impact of the virus, which was devastating in China and other areas of Southeast Asia. HIV/AIDS among injecting drug users is increasingly becoming a concern for international organizations. At the moment, the level of HIV is less than 0.1 percent of the population, but this could easily rise if nothing is done to prevent the spread of the disease.

Indoor pollution is a major health problem, with half of all Indonesian homes burning biomass fuels – such as wood, charcoal, and animal droppings – to cook with. The smoke from these fuels causes respiratory problems and has been linked to low birth weights and some types of cancer.

EDUCATION

Education improved during the Suharto period and continues to do so today. In 2002, literacy rates for the whole population reached 83 percent for women and 92 percent for men. Because of conflict and neglect of facilities, however, 30 percent of

primary schools in Indonesia have been destroyed or are beyond repair. In Aceh, for example, many children have to be taught in tents or mosques instead.

Officially education for Indonesian children is compulsory for nine years, but the reality is very different. Despite high enrollment rates for primary schools, three in every four children will not start or complete secondary school. There are immense economic pressures for older children to find paid employment to help support their families, or to tend crops on family land. Keeping children in school can be difficult for poorer families.

Private schools are popular with those who can afford the fees. Christian schools have a very high reputation and accept children of other faiths. Since 20003, every Indonesian school is required by law to teach each student about his or her own religion – for example, Muslim children in Christian schools are taught about Islam.

RELIGION

When Indonesia gained independence, one of the country's guiding principles was the belief in a supreme god. People could freely choose their official religion, even if they did not practice it, as long as it was either Islam, Hinduism, Buddhism, Confucianism or Christianity. Christianity is the newest of these religions in the archipelago – arriving with the Portuguese. However, other religions have since been acknowledged, such as the Toraja religion in 1969 and the Dayak religion, Kaharigan, in 1983.

Indonesia is home to the world's largest Muslim population. Here, practicing Muslims are called *santri*. For many Muslim families the

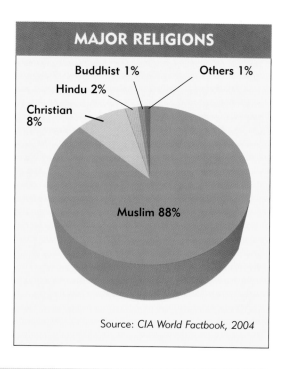

MAJOR RELIGIONS

Buddhist 1%   Others 1%
Hindu 2%
Christian 8%
Muslim 88%

Source: *CIA World Factbook, 2004*

The festival of Nyepi is especially important for Balinese Hindus, marking the end of the old year and the beginning of the new. The day before Nyepi, there are big celebrations and great activity. In the evening, people chase away evil spirits with loud noise, flaming torches and bonfires. On the day of Nyepi, people do nothing. This is to make any returning evil spirits think Bali is deserted and move elsewhere. This brings prosperity for the new year.

The *ogoh-ogoh* effigy is burnt on bonfires in the evening before Nyepi.

mosque provides more than a place of worship. It is a place where social organizations meet, children are taught Arabic and religious studies, and charitable donations are distributed to the poor. Many of the Islamic customs in Indonesia differ from those in some other Islamic countries – creating greater social freedoms, especially for women. Although Islam and Islamic groups have played important roles in politics, Indonesia continues to be a secular (nonreligious) state.

The island of Bali is mainly Hindu. It differs from Indian or Nepali Hinduism in that the Balinese Hindus have a supreme god called Sanghyang Widi. Balinese gods and spirits have daily importance and offerings are made for good fortune and luck. There is a caste system, but its main significance is in religious roles and rituals, rather than the division of labor as in India.

Animism, the worship of spirits and ancestors, is still widespread in Indonesia. It remains the dominant form of worship in isolated regions of Kalimantan, Papua and Samba. In other areas, it continues to form the basis of many people's daily lives, regardless of their religion.

WOMEN'S LIVES

Women have essential roles within Indonesian life beyond traditional family responsibilities. Women have always been active in agriculture – though often this has been for subsistence and not paid employment. The female economic contribution to the family has often been underestimated, though women have a long history of producing and selling goods in markets. Today, women are becoming better educated and more are entering the labor force, especially in manufacturing industries. Women are getting married later and, in Java especially, are older when they start having children.

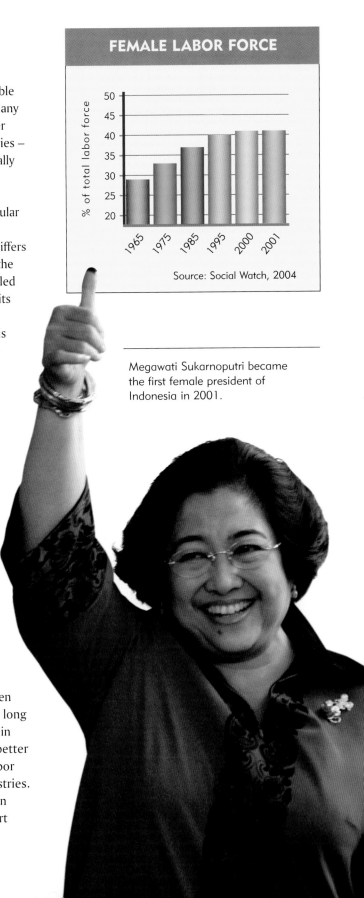

FEMALE LABOR FORCE

% of total labor force

Source: Social Watch, 2004

Megawati Sukarnoputri became the first female president of Indonesia in 2001.

FOOD

Rice is the staple (main) food for much of Indonesia. Plain rice is usually cooked in the morning, along with three or four other dishes. These are left in the home for people to eat throughout the day. Chili sauce called *sambal* accompanies most meals. Most people eat with their right hands and not with utensils as is done in other parts of the world. Indonesians are famous for grazing throughout the day, rather than eating just two or three larger meals. Many people can be seen enjoying *sate* (grilled meat on bamboo skewers), *gado gado* (vegetable salad with peanut sauce) and other dishes, which they buy from street vendors during the day.

Farther east the land becomes progressively less fertile and drier, and here the root vegetables cassava and taro, along with sago and corn, replace rice as the staple foodstuff. Throughout the islands, fish and seafood provide an important source of protein. There is a great variety of local specialties throughout the islands. Some, like bats in chili, are a little more unusual than others.

RECREATION

Badminton is one of the most popular sports in Indonesia. The national team is very successful in international competitions. Many Indonesians follow regional and international soccer teams. Often in the evenings, after work or school, people can be seen playing badminton or soccer on the streets. Indonesia also has its own martial art called *pencak silat*, which is most popular in Sumatra and Java. Areas with histories of tribal warfare often have traditional fighting contests and demonstrations at festivals and special ceremonies.

Indonesia has a strong tradition of music, dance and theater. The traditional *gamelan* orchestras are made up of percussion

People stop to buy a snack from the *sate* sellers at the roadside in Yogyakarta.

Dynamic players in a match held in Jakarta.

CASE STUDY
Sepak Takraw

Also known as *sepak raga*, the game of *sepak takraw* is played throughout Southeast Asia, mainly by men. It is a spectacular mix of volleyball and soccer played with a rattan ball.

Players dive around the court to keep the ball off the ground, trying to return it over the high net. They are not allowed to use their hands, except to drop the ball onto the foot to serve. Players launch themselves up into the air to perform amazing kicks in an attempt to win a point.

instruments, such as metal gongs and drums, along with flutes and xylophones. *Dangdut* is a form of Indonesian music, often about love and romance, which mixes the *gamelan* with modern music.

Dance ranges from the nightclubs of Jakarta or Kuta to the Mandua dance with knives in Kalimantan or the ballet in Yogyakarta. Dance and drama are closely related, with many dances telling stories. The quest of Prince Rama to find his kidnapped wife is told in the *Ramayana* dances. This is also a popular story for *wayang* puppetry. The leather shadow puppets – *wayang kulit* – are made from the hides of water buffaloes. The ornate wooden puppets – *wayang golek* – show the talented craft skills of people throughout Indonesia.

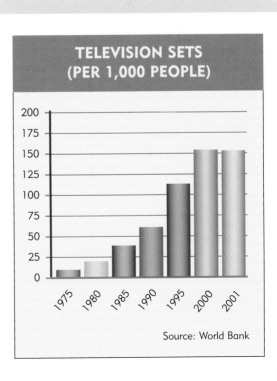

TELEVISION SETS (PER 1,000 PEOPLE)

Source: World Bank

The Javan rhinoceros is now endangered through poaching and habitat destruction.

Indonesia's biodiversity (variety of plant and animal species) reflects its position between Asia and Australia – having species from both continents. The archipelago is home to more than 25 percent of the world's fish, 17 percent of birds, 16 percent of reptiles and amphibians, 12 percent of mammals and 10 percent of all flowering plant species. But this environment is under constant threat from the many pressures of expanding industry and daily life.

BRIDGING ASIA AND AUSTRALIA

In the 1850s, the British naturalist Alfred Russel Wallace surveyed the plant and animal life in Sulawesi and Borneo. Although the two islands were close and had the same climate, he noticed they had important differences in their wildlife. In 1859, Wallace proposed the archipelago could be divided into two areas – the Asian in the west and the Australian in the east. Wallace's line (see the map opposite) marked the boundary between the two – heading from south of the Philippines between Borneo and Sulawesi, and dividing Bali and Lombok. Further surveys have created other lines dividing the islands' wildlife, such as Weber's line (intended to replace Wallace's line) and Lydekker's line (considered the boundary of marsupials). Sulawesi, Maluku and Nusa Tenggara are seen as a transition area between the wildlife of the two continents, sometimes called Wallacea.

On the savannah plains of Papua, bush wallabies are found, and in its vast forests there are four species of tree kangaroos. Echidnas and other marsupial animals all make Papua their home. The birdwing butterfly lives on Papua, and with a wingspan of 33cm (13 inches), it is the largest butterfly in Southeast Asia. Amazingly, half of all the plants and animals found in Papua are not found anywhere outside of the island of New Guinea.

On the islands of Sumatra, Borneo and Java, there are many animals related to species in mainland Asia. Tigers, elephants, rhinoceroses and leopards still exist, but in declining numbers. Land use has changed over time, reducing the area covered by forest, especially on densely populated Java. Sumatra and Borneo are home to the orangutan, the only great ape found outside of Africa. Many conservation projects are trying to increase populations of endangered species.

NUMBER OF SPECIES IN INDONESIA, 2002

	NUMBER OF SPECIES	NUMBER OF THREATENED SPECIES
Mammals	515	147
Birds*	929	114
Flowering plants	29,375	384

* with breeding range in Indonesia

WALLACE'S, WEBER'S AND LYDEKKER'S LINES

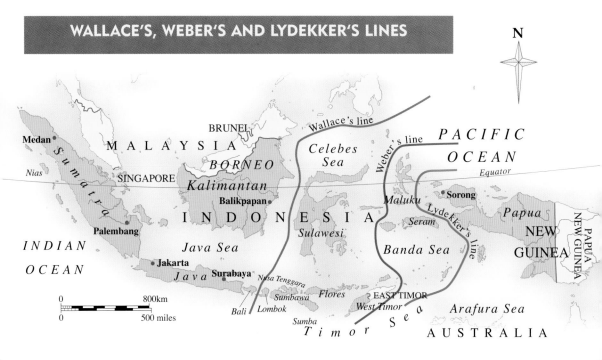

INDONESIA'S GIANT FLOWERS

Indonesia is home to a variety of giant flowers. The *Rafflesia arnoldi* is the world's largest single flower, growing up to a width of 1m. It is a parasitic plant, taking its nutrients from the plants on which it grows. The *Amorphophallus titanium* is the world's largest individual flower cluster. The plant only blooms every three to four years and can reach 3.3m tall. Both of these plants have a foul smell of rotting meat when they are in full bloom.

The *Rafflesia arnoldi* blooms between August and November.

COASTAL AND MARINE ENVIRONMENTS

Indonesia is home to 30 percent of the world's mangrove forests, with more than 33 species of mangroves. Around Merauke on Papua, these swamps extend for 300km inland from the coast. The proboscis monkey, one of the many primates in Indonesia, inhabits the coastal forests of Kalimantan and Sumatra. It is very distinctive with its large bulbous nose.

Along with the Philippines and Malaysia, Indonesia forms part of the Coral Triangle – a region with one of the world's most diverse and important coastal and marine ecosystems. In Indonesian waters alone there are over 400 different species of coral. The reefs are home to some of the most beautiful fish in the world, including the clownfish, damselfish, wrasse and twin spot coris. Many of these are caught and sold abroad – to supply the demand for exotic and ornamental fish. The red and golden-red Asian Bonytongue (or Asian Arowana) was the most sought-after ornamental fish for collectors, and prices could fetch thousands of dollars. The trade in this fish was banned worldwide in 1975, and they became a protected species in Indonesia in 1980. Pearl oysters are found in Indonesia, and they are highly valued for their large size and high quality.

Five of the seven species of sea turtles are found in Indonesian waters – the leatherback, Olive Ridley, loggerhead, hawksbill and green. Green turtles have been heavily exploited, with eggs taken and turtles killed for their meat and shells. There are also 22 species of marine mammals. Dolphin-watching, off the north coast of Bali, is becoming a popular activity for tourists. This form of ecotourism provides an important income for many local people, while encouraging the preservation of the ecosystem through sustainable use.

Local fishermen take tourists dolphin-watching in Bali to earn extra money.

The Komodo dragon uses its keen sense of smell to find prey.

The islands of Komodo, Padar and Rinca are home to the world's largest lizard. Locals call it the *ora*, but it is more commonly known as the Komodo dragon. It is a protected species and the national animal of Indonesia. Komodo dragons can grow up to 3m long and weigh more than 70kg. To avoid being eaten, the young live in trees. When they are too large they find holes to shelter in.

Komodo dragons like to eat dead or decaying flesh – preferring the Timor deer – but they are not fussy and will even eat each other. They often ambush prey, killing them with their strong claws and sharp teeth. If not killed outright, the prey is likely to die from blood poisoning within a week from the lizard's septic saliva. The Komodo dragon can eat up to 80 percent of its body weight in a single meal. This is important, since it is an opportunist feeder – if there is no food then it can go for days without eating. Large meals can take up to a week to digest.

Workers stand on illegally sawn timber. Illegal logging is destroying the Indonesian forests.

THREATS TO THE ENVIRONMENT

Indonesia faces a range of threats to the environment through the changing uses of the land and the misuse and overuse of resources. Illegal logging is a major problem, with deforestation measured at an average of $13,124km^2$ per year between 1990 and 2000.

The mining of coral and coral rocks for cement and the construction industry is destroying the reefs, which provide a natural defense against the sea – so rates of coastal erosion are climbing fast. In Candidasa in Bali, the beach disappeared after the destruction of the reef.

The marine and coastal ecosystems are also under threat from unsustainable fishing practices. Blast fishing, cyanide fishing, the use of traps and reef gleaning all destroy coral and the habitat of fish. Overfishing has caused stock numbers to rapidly decline. Water pollution, including untreated waste, can smother the corals and kill them.

POSITIVE SOLUTIONS

A number of positive steps have been taken at the local, national and international levels to protect the environment. There are $373,200km^2$ of national protected land – 20.6 percent of the total land area, and an increase from 7.6 percent in 1985. National parks and marine reserves not only offer protection to the diverse species of Indonesia, they also provide an opportunity for research and ecotourism. Orangutan conservation in Kalimantan and Sumatra is one such example.

The government has also taken steps to reduce the destructive impact of industries. The reduction in logging areas, new limits on open-pit mining and a ban on the clearing of land by fire are three examples.

International pressure can help promote sustainable use of materials within Indonesia. In early 2004, the British government banned plywood imports from Indonesia, based on reports that 80 percent was produced from illegally logged trees. This had immediate effect: The Indonesian government began inspecting factories and issued licences to those using only legal materials.

KALIMANTAN FOREST FIRES

Fires raged out of control in Kalimantan in 1997, and again in 1998. A haze developed over the island, spreading to Singapore and Malaysia. Plantation owners and indigenous groups using swidden (slash-and-burn) agriculture started fires to clear land, and these got out of control. This was made worse by the effects of El Niño, which caused unusually dry conditions. The fires caused widespread damage to the environment and increased respiratory illnesses among people affected by the haze.

CASE STUDY
GUNUNG LEUSER NATIONAL PARK

Increasing orangutan numbers will take time because adult females produce few young.

The Gunung Leuser National Park in northern Sumatra is home to the endangered Sumatran species of rhinoceros, tiger and orangutan. Many people believe this is the last place in Sumatra where wild populations of these species can be increased through conservation projects.

The region is under threat – illegal logging is destroying habitats and causing an increase in mudslides as the protective canopy is lost. Illegal logging, mudslides and adverse weather conditions have been blamed for the flash flooding of Bukit Lawang, on the edge of the national park, in 2003 – over 200 people were killed. A major road-building project meant to link Aceh with the rest of Sumatra threatens to destroy more of the national park.

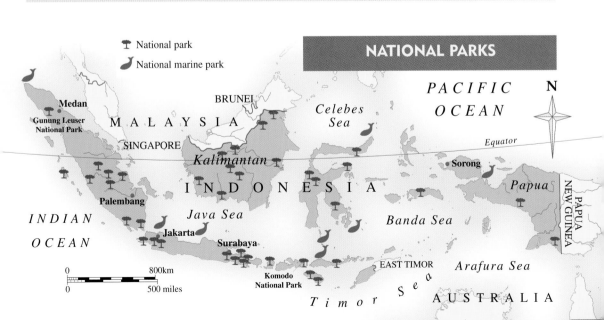

NATIONAL PARKS

🌳 National park

🐋 National marine park

Medan
Gunung Leuser National Park
BRUNEI
Celebes Sea
PACIFIC OCEAN
N

MALAYSIA
SINGAPORE
Equator
Kalimantan
Sorong
INDONESIA
Papua
PAPUA NEW GUINEA

Palembang
Java Sea
Banda Sea
INDIAN OCEAN
Jakarta
Surabaya

0 ——— 800km
0 ——— 500 miles
Komodo National Park
EAST TIMOR
Arafura Sea
Timor Sea
AUSTRALIA

Scavenging for items in the waste dumped in an Indonesian river.

INDUSTRIAL AND URBAN POLLUTION

Pollution is a major problem in Indonesia. Respiratory diseases are the sixth-largest cause of death in the country, and many of these could be avoided if air pollution were reduced. Urban areas, where industries and motor vehicles are most concentrated, tend to be the worst affected. Between 1995 and 2000, the number of vehicles in Indonesia increased from 12 million to almost 21 million, and the numbers keep rising. Carbon dioxide emissions, which are linked with global warming, have increased by over 271 percent since 1980, with 87.1 million tonnes produced in 2001. Much of these emissions come from generating power for both industry and domestic use. Almost 87 percent of energy in Indonesia is produced by the burning of fossil fuels (gas 34 percent, coal 29 percent and oil 24 percent). Air pollution will worsen unless renewable sources are used. Today, only 4 percent of Indonesia's massive geothermal potential is being harnessed.

The government is trying to ban leaded gasoline throughout Indonesia to cut lead pollution. However, the state-owned oil company Pertamina is not yet able to produce enough unleaded fuel. Since the economic crisis there has been a lack of funding for the necessary upgrading of the refineries.

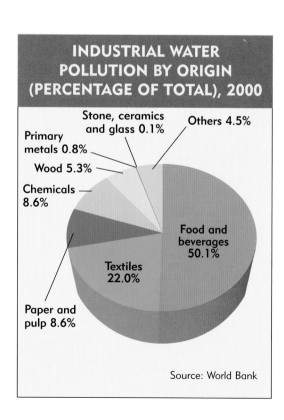

INDUSTRIAL WATER POLLUTION BY ORIGIN (PERCENTAGE OF TOTAL), 2000

Stone, ceramics and glass 0.1%
Others 4.5%
Primary metals 0.8%
Wood 5.3%
Chemicals 8.6%
Food and beverages 50.1%
Textiles 22.0%
Paper and pulp 8.6%

Source: World Bank

Indonesia uses around 75 billion cubic meters of water a year, which is taken from the rivers, lakes and underground reservoirs. The widespread use of unregulated agricultural chemicals is causing serious ecological damage as these find their way into larger ecosystems. Many factories have reportedly been dumping untreated waste materials into local rivers.

Although sanitation is improving in many areas, the level of water contamination caused by sewage is high. A study in Jakarta found that 90 percent of the shallow groundwater wells were polluted with domestic waste in 2001. Seawater contaminating drinking water supplies is a major problem in coastal towns and cities as the local water table lowers due to overuse.

CASE STUDY
TRAFFIC POLLUTION IN JAKARTA

Jakarta has one of the most polluted atmospheres in the world. Many of the 5 million vehicles in the city are scooters and motorcycles without catalytic converters, which lower harmful emissions. Lead pollution is a problem. In one study, a third of children had levels of lead in their blood high enough to cause learning and concentration problems. Unleaded gas is being phased in throughout Indonesia and more rapidly in Jakarta. But the city authorities only have the power to enforce these regulations with public vehicles, which account for little over 6 percent of Jakarta's traffic.

The authorities introduced a "three-in-one" policy, which required each car to have at least three people in it when driving into the city center. It has not been very successful in cutting the number of cars. Instead, many Indonesians make money from it. They line the roads leading into the center, and drivers without enough passengers pick them up and pay them for the short trip into the controlled area.

Measures need to be taken to reduce pollution within Jakarta.

53

Poverty and the lack of basic services continue to be major problems.

Indonesia is a spectacular country, diverse in landscape and people. It has amazing potential to grow into a wealthy and prosperous nation. Yet it faces many challenges on the road ahead. Among them are the questions of national unity, the control of natural resources, the importance of the environment and the need to reduce poverty.

REGIONAL QUESTIONS

"Unity in diversity," or *bhinneka tunggal ika* as they say in Indonesia (see page 30), is being tested. Since the mid-1970s, the government in Jakarta has been facing calls for independence in distant provinces, including Aceh in Sumatra, and Papua. Independence has not been granted and violent confrontation has continued. Efforts at finding peace have not led to any long-term solutions.

The government recently started a program of decentralization. This gives greater powers to regional, provincial and district-level decision makers over everyday issues. It is hoped this will reduce conflict as people work together on improving conditions in their areas. Supporters of decentralization argue that it extends democracy, involving more people in decision making.

On the other hand, there are many people who are opposed to regional autonomy and decentralization. Some say there are not enough resources and qualified people to run the extra layers of government. Others argue that the rampant corruption that plagues Indonesia will only increase: Small powerful groups will dominate councils, using them to further their own interests. Violence has already occurred due to unrepresentative local politics and decentralization may increase conflict.

There is also the issue of who controls what resources. Not all areas in Indonesia have access to the same raw materials or size of workforce. Many people fear there will be a growing division between resource-rich areas and areas with few resources. President Yudhoyono faces a very difficult job in stamping out corruption and maintaining a unified nation.

POVERTY AND INEQUALITY

There are vast differences in wealth in Indonesia and access to resources. While the number of people using the Internet is increasing, almost half the population is still without electricity. Access to basic services, such as sanitation, would improve the quality of life for large numbers of people. Drinking water would not become infected and people would suffer fewer diarrheal diseases. These diseases are still a major cause of death in Indonesia.

If poverty can be reduced further, then Indonesia's potential has a greater chance of being fulfilled. One of the problems with poverty is that it often forces children out of school. Education is crucial, especially if the country wants to develop more highly skilled workers in new sectors of industry, which will help the economy grow.

TELECOMMUNICATIONS DATA, 2002 (PER 1,000 PEOPLE)	
Mainline phones	37
Mobile phones	55
Internet users	38

Source: World Bank

THE ECONOMY

The Indonesian economy is beginning to grow after the crisis in 1997, but it is vulnerable to changes in the global economy. International agreements have in the past protected Indonesian industries. With some of these agreements ending – for example, for textiles – unemployment is likely to increase as Indonesia struggles to keep up with other competitors. Indonesia needs to increase the range of products and services it supplies to remain internationally competitive. Tourism has major potential to provide new jobs and economic growth.

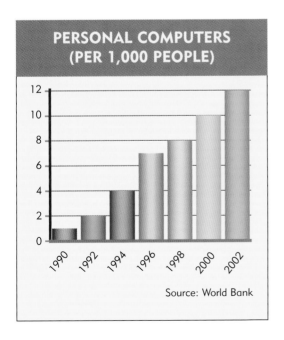

PERSONAL COMPUTERS (PER 1,000 PEOPLE)

Source: World Bank

Internet use is increasing within Indonesia, mainly in the cities.

BALANCING THE ECONOMY AND THE ENVIRONMENT

Expanding ecotourism supports the economy while protecting the environment.

The big question facing Indonesia is how best to use the country's natural resources to improve people's standard of living while protecting the environment. It is not an easy situation, and it confronts many developing countries. Countries must often make compromises between people and the environment, and it is essential that they reach a balance – protecting globally important ecosystems and improving people's quality of life.

Sustainable management of resources is needed, but it involves more than passing laws saying how much forest can be cleared, or what practices can be used. Indonesia needs to enforce these laws, or else illegal logging and fishing will destroy ecosystems that have developed over millions of years. Renewable sources need to be managed sensibly for the long term, so they are continually available for use.

Indonesia has huge potential to expand geothermal, hydroelectric (HEP) and solar energy production. Lowering the dependency on fossil fuels will cut pollution and help reduce the growing carbon dioxide emissions, which are linked with global warming. It is a critical time for the environment and unity of the archipelago. Wasted chances could turn a bright future bleak.

THE UNKNOWN

Not all the events that affect Indonesia can be controlled. It is an archipelago of volcanoes and geological instability. The active volcanoes are monitored and plans are in place to evacuate people close by, if necessary. But homes and livelihoods cannot be evacuated, and these can be wiped out with one blast.

The Asian tsunami on December 26, 2004 and the earthquake off the island of Nias on March 28, 2005 demonstrated the unpredictability of natural events, and devastation only takes minutes. Nature's power has created major obstacles to the country's development and can do so again. Indonesia's challenge is to overcome them.

CASE STUDY
THE ASIAN TSUNAMI:
DESTRUCTION AND RECONSTRUCTION

On December 26, 2004, an undersea earthquake just kilometers off the Sumatran coast caused tsunami, or giant sea waves. Within minutes towns were flattened by the giant waves. The north tip and west coast of Sumatra were devastated. More than 125,000 people were confirmed dead. Tens of thousands more are missing, presumed dead, and the livelihoods of those remaining were destroyed in what has been described as one of the worst humanitarian disasters in modern times.

Aceh was hit the hardest by the tsunami, but not only because of nature's destructive power. The ability to respond to a crisis and to rebuild lives afterward is shaped by social and political forces. Aceh is the scene of a violent conflict between the Indonesian military and separatist groups that has taken about 13,000 lives since 1976. Concern for the safety of relief workers initially caused the military to limit the movement of aid organizations. After a cease-fire was reached, relief efforts were set up throughout the province. It is uncertain whether the issues that caused the conflict can be resolved without a return to violence.

Because poverty and unemployment are exceptionally high in the wake of the tsunami, many donors have given money to reconstruct infrastructure, towns and livelihoods. But corruption threatens to take those essential

Standing amid the devastation in Aceh. The challenges of reconstruction lie ahead.

funds away from the people who need them most. How quickly and successfully corruption is tackled will shape the future of Aceh and the rest of Indonesia – for the better or worse.

Arable land Land used for or suitable for temporary crops. It does not include land abandoned as a result of swidden agriculture.

Archipelago A group of islands.

Autonomy The condition of being self-governing, rather than administered by the central government.

Blast fishing The use of explosives to stun fish so they are easier to catch. This practice destroys coral reefs.

Continental shelf A flat or gently sloping section of the continental land found below sea level, forming an extension to the coastal plain. There is a sheer drop at the edge of the shelf where it meets deep ocean.

Cyanide fishing A fishing method that uses cyanide, a poison, to tranquilize fish. The poison damages the coral and the marine ecosystem.

Decentralization The process by which the government gives more power to the provinces and districts to look after their own affairs.

Ecosystem The relationship between interacting living organisms and their physical environment. An ecosystem can be tiny or as large as planet Earth.

Ecotourism Tourism that is sensitive to its impact on the environment and people.

El Niño A phenomenon of the tropical Pacific Ocean that brings heavy wet weather to normally dry areas and severe dry conditions to normally rainy areas. It usually occurs once every four to eight years.

GDP (gross domestic product) The monetary value of goods and services produced by a country in a year.

Geothermal power Energy gained from the internal heat of the Earth. Volcanoes and hot springs are great sources of this energy, which can be used to produce electricity.

GNI (gross national income) The monetary value of goods and services produced by a country, plus any income from earnings overseas by the country's citizens, in a single year. It used to be called gross national product (GNP).

Irrigate To deliberately supply farmland with water. One example is controlled flooding, which is used for rice cultivation.

Kampong The Malay word for "village." The term is used to describe small settlements usually of poor housing in deprived areas.

Marginal poor The group of people whose income is just above the poverty line. These people could easily fall below the line if changes happen in their lives, such as illness or the loss of a job.

Militia A nongovernment military force.

Naturalist An expert in the natural history of plants and animals.

Ocean trench A large, linear depression formed in the ocean floor where subduction of tectonic plates occurs. They are usually 50 to 100km wide and several thousand meters deep.

Permanent cropland Land that is used for crops that occupy the land for long periods of time and do not need to be replanted after each harvest. Coffee, cocoa and rubber are all examples of such crops.

Population density The number of people living in a certain area of land.

Poverty line A measurement of poverty. All the people who have a daily income less than a certain value, for example US$1, are said to be below the poverty line.

Purchasing Power Parity (PPP) The calculation made to some national statistics so they can be compared with other countries accurately.

Reef gleaning A destructive method of fishing that scrapes away coral to gain access to fish and other marine animals. It creates large areas of dead reef.

Relative humidity The ratio of the moisture in the air to the amount of moisture the air could hold at a certain temperature, expressed as a percentage.

Separatists People who want independence from a country so they can form their own nation.

Services Economic activities that are paid for, although no physical product is made. This includes tourism, banking, health and education.

Subduction The movement of one tectonic plate underneath another one as they move toward each other.

Subsistence The production of enough food and other goods to meet the needs of the household without producing excess that could be sold.

Sustainable Describing methods used to make sure something continues to exist, or happen, for a long time.

Swidden agriculture A traditional farming method in which land is cleared and the debris is burned so it can be used to grow crops, after which it is left to regenerate naturally; also called slash-and-burn farming.

Tectonic plates Large sections of the Earth's crust that move slowly over the Earth's molten mantle.

Transmigration (*transmigrasi*) The policy of moving people from a densely populated area to one that is less populated.

Tsunami Giant sea waves caused by movements in the Earth's surface, such as undersea earthquakes.

FURTHER INFORMATION

BOOKS TO READ:

Cochrane, Janet, and Gerald Cubitt. *The National Parks and Other Wild Places of Indonesia.* London: New Holland, 2000. A beautiful collection of photographs of the plants and animals of Indonesia.

Cribb, Robert. *Historical Atlas of Indonesia.* Honolulu: University of Hawaii Press, 2000. A book with useful chapters on the archipelago's changing geology and landscape, along with many illustrative maps.

Daws, Gavan, and Marty Fujita. *Archipelago: Islands of Indonesia.* Berkeley: University of California Press, 1999. A richly illustrated book tracing the historic biological tour of the 19th-century naturalist Alfred Russel Wallace.

Witton, Patrick. *Lonely Planet Travel Guide to Indonesia.* 7th ed. Footscray, Victoria, Australia: Lonely Planet, 2003. A comprehensive guide to traveling in Indonesia.

WEBSITES:

GENERAL INFORMATION AND STATISTICS

CIA World Factbook
http://www.cia.gov/cia/publications/factbook/geos/id.html
Statistics and assessments of all the countries in the world.

Indonesian Central Bureau of Statistics
http://www.bps.go.id/
Official statistics on Indonesia.

DEVELOPMENT
United Nations Development Program
http://www.undp.or.id/
Information on international projects in Indonesia, including tsunami relief efforts.

WILDLIFE AND NATIONAL PARKS

Komodo National Park
http://www.komodonationalpark.org
Facts about the park and species that live in it.

Sumatran Orangutan Society
http://orangutans-sos.org/
Information about the Sumatran orangutan.

WWF (World Wildlife Fund)
http://wwf.org/
A gateway to the WWF's conservation projects worldwide, including protection of Indonesia's coral reefs.

METRIC CONVERSION TABLE

To convert	to	do this
mm (millimeters)	inches	divide by 25.4
cm (centimeters)	inches	divide by 2.54
m (meters)	feet	multiply by 3.281
m (meters)	yards	multiply by 1.094
km (kilometers)	yards	multiply by 1094
km (kilometers)	miles	divide by 1.6093
kilometers per hour	miles per hour	divide by 1.6093
cm^2 (square centimeters)	square inches	divide by 6.452
m^2 (square meters)	square feet	multiply by 10.76
m^2 (square meters)	square yards	multiply by 1.196
km^2 (square kilometers)	square miles	divide by 2.59
km^2 (square kilometers)	acres	multiply by 247.1
hectares	acres	multiply by 2.471
cm^3 (cubic centimeters)	cubic inches	multiply by 16.387
m^3 (cubic meters)	cubic yards	multiply by 1.308
l (liters)	pints	multiply by 2.113
l (liters)	gallons	divide by 3.785
g (grams)	ounces	divide by 28.329
kg (kilograms)	pounds	multiply by 2.205
metric tonnes	short tons	multiply by 1.1023
metric tonnes	long tons	multiply by 0.9842
BTUs (British thermal units)	kWh (kilowatt-hours)	divide by 3,415.3
watts	horsepower	multiply by 0.001341
kWh (kilowatt-hours)	horsepower-hours	multiply by 1.341
MW (megawatts)	horsepower	multiply by 1,341
gigawatts per hour	horsepower per hour	multiply by 1,341,000
°C (degrees Celsius)	°F (degrees Fahrenheit)	multiply by 1.8 then add 32

Numbers shown in **bold** refer to pages with maps, graphic illustrations or photographs.

agriculture *(see also rice, spice trade)* 24
  history 10
  pollution 53
  spices **11**
  swidden 30, 50, 59
  women 43
animals *(see also wildlife)* 9, **46**, **47**, **48**, **49**
  conservation 50

Bali **9**, **17**
  agriculture 10, 24, **25**
  animals 48
  bombing **28**, 37
  coastal erosion 50
  history 10
  population 32, 34, **35**
  religion 43
  volcanoes 14, 15
beaches **8**
Borneo 16, **17**, 46
Buddhism **10**, **42**

Christianity *(see also religion)* 37, 41, **42**
climate *(see also weather)* 14, **18**, 46
coal 9, 22, **23**, 52
coral reefs **8**, **16**, 48, 50

diseases 38, 55
droughts 18

East Timor **9**, **13**
economy 9, 20, 29, 31, 34, 55, **56**
  conflicts 36
  Suharto 13
  urbanization 35
ecotourism 29, 48, 50, **56**, 58
education 21, 33, **41**, 43, 55
electrical products 20, 27
ethnic groups 9, 30, 31, 37
exports *(see also economy)* 20, **21**, 22, 26, 27

fishing industry 26, 50, 56
flooding **18**, 51

forests *(see also rain forests)* 26, 34, **50**
  management 56
  mangroves 48
  mining **22**
  products 9
  wildlife 46

gas 9, 20, 21, **23**
  pollution 52
GDP (gross domestic product) *(see also economy)* 9, 20, **24**, 58
glaciers 14
GNI (gross national income) *(see also economy)* **21**, 58

habitat destruction 9, **46**, 50, 51
health 21, 40
Hinduism *(see also religion)* 10, **42**, 43
housing 38, 39

imports *(see also economy)* 20, **21**, 24
independence 9, 12, 31, **36**, 42, 54
industry 20, 24, 28, 32, **52**, 55
  environment 46, 50
  urbanization 35
  women **43**
Islam *(see also Muslims, religion)* 10, 28, 37, 41, 42, 43

Jakarta **9**
  climate 18, **19**
  government 54
  pollution **53**
  poor **38**, 39
  population **34**, **35**
  wood products **26**
Java **9**, **10**, 16, **17**
  agriculture 10, 24
  climate 18
  history 10
  population 9, **30**, 32, 34, **35**
  sports 44
  volcanoes 14
  wildlife 46
  women 43
Java Man 10
Java Trench 16

kampongs 38, **39**, 58
Komodo dragon **49**
Krakatau **15**

languages 9, 30, 31
life expectancy **40**
logging 9, 27, **50**, 51, 56

Maluku **9**, 16
  climate 18
  population **35**
  volcanoes 8, 14
  wildlife 46
mangroves 16, **33**, 48
metals 9, 20, 22, **52**
minerals 23
mining **22**, **23**, 50
mountains 14, 19
music 8, 44, **45**
Muslims *(see also Islam, religion)* 8, **12**, 32, 37, 41, **42**

national parks 50, **51**
Nusa Tenggara **9**, 16
  climate 18
  population **35**
  volcanoes 8, 14
  wildlife 46

oil 9, **20**, 21, **23**, 52

Padang **9**, **19**
paper 20, 27, **52**
Papua **9**, 16, **17**
  decentralization 54
  mangroves 48
  migration 34
  mining 23
  population 9, 34, **35**
  religion 43
  tectonic plates 14
  wildlife 46
Peranakan people **31**
plants 9, 46, **47**
pollution 9, 22, **52**, 56
  air 41, 52, **53**
  water 38, 50, **52**, 53
population 8, 9, 32, 33, **34**, **35**, 58
  conflicts 36
  growth 24

Casting a fishing net on the beach in Mentiggi, Lombok.

poverty 9, 13, 20, 33, 38, **39, 54,** 55, 57

power generation 20, **21,** 52, 56

rainfall, *(see also climate)* **18, 19**

rain forests *(see also forests)* 18, 19, 23

religion 36, 37, 38, 41, **42,** 43

resources 9, 26
  conflicts 36
  decentralization 54, 55
  management 56
  threats 50

rice 10, 24, **25,** 44

roads *(see also transportation)* **29**

service industries 21, **24,** 28, 35, 59

services 38, 39, **54,** 55

ships *(see also transportation)* 29

spice trade 11, 24

sports 44, **45**

subduction 14, 16, 59

Suharto (president) 12, 13, 32, 41

Sukarno (president) 12, 32

Sukarnoputri, Megawati (president) 13, **43**

Sulawesi **9, 16, 17**
  ceremonies 31
  climate **19**
  conflicts 37
  population **35**
  volcanoes 8, 14, 46

Sumatra **9, 16, 17**
  animals 48
  conservation 50, 51
  decentralization 54
  migration 34
  population **35**
  sports 44
  tsunami 57
  volcanoes 8, 14, 15
  wildlife 46

tectonic plates 14, 16, 59

telecommunications 20, **55**

temperature *(see also climate)* 18, **19**

terrorism **28,** 37

textiles 20, **27, 52,** 55

tourism 21, 28, 29, **48,** 50, 55, **56**

transmigration 24, 31, 34, 36, **37,** 59

transportation 20, **29**

tsunami 15, 57, 59

unemployment **26,** 29, 33, 35, 38, 55, 57

volcanoes 8, 14, **15,** 17, 57

Wallace, Alfred Russel 46

weather *(see also climate)* 14, 51

wildlife 8, 46, 48, **51**

wood products 20, **26,** 27, **52**

Yudhoyono, Susilo Bambang (president) 13, 55